D1279888

THE GIFT OF
happiness

THE GIFT OF
happiness

sophie bevan

RYLAND
PETERS
& SMALL

LONDON NEW YORK

Designer Pamela Daniels

Senior Editor Clare Double

Picture Research Claire Hector

Production Patricia Harrington

Art Director Gabriella Le Grazie

Publishing Director Alison Starling

First published in the
United States in 2004
by Ryland Peters & Small, Inc.
519 Broadway, 5th Floor
New York NY 10012
www.rylandpeters.com

10 9 8 7 6 5 4 3 2

Text, design, and photographs
© Ryland Peters & Small 2004

ISBN 1 84172 735 0

Printed and bound in China

contents

the search

If you ever find happiness by hunting for it, you will find it, as the old woman did her lost spectacles, safe on her own nose all the time.

JOSH BILLINGS (1818–1885)

Happiness

depends, as Nature shows,
Less on exterior things than
most suppose.

WILLIAM COWPER (1731–1800)

To find the Eternal Way is the only happiness.

CEN CAN (715–770), *ASCENDING THE PAGODA AT THE TEMPLE OF KIND FAVOR WITH GAO SHI AND XUE JU*

The Declaration of Independence only guarantees the American people the right to pursue happiness. You have to catch it yourself.

BENJAMIN FRANKLIN (1706–1790)

It's not money that brings happiness, it's lots of money.

RUSSIAN SAYING

Real happiness is cheap enough, yet how dearly we pay for its counterfeit.

HOSEA BALLOU THE 2ND (1796–1861)

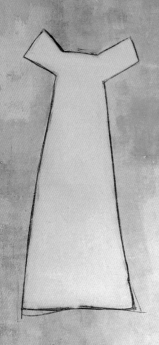

If solid happiness we prize,
Within our breast this
  jewel lies,
And they are fools who roam.
The world has nothing to
  bestow;
From our own selves our joys
  must flow,
And that dear hut, our home.

NATHANIEL COTTON (1707–1788), *THE FIRESIDE*

Why go farther and farther,
Look, happiness is right here.
Learn how to grab hold of luck,
For luck is always there.

JOHANN WOLFGANG VON GOETHE (1749–1832), *REMEMBRANCE*

Happiness

is like a butterfly
which, when pursued,
is always beyond our
grasp, but, if you will
sit down quietly, may
alight upon you.

NATHANIEL HAWTHORNE (1804–1864),
THE SCARLET LETTER

Happiness grows at our own firesides, and is not to be picked in strangers' gardens.

DOUGLAS JERROLD (1803–1857)

But does not happiness come from the soul within?

HONORÉ DE BALZAC (1799–1850)

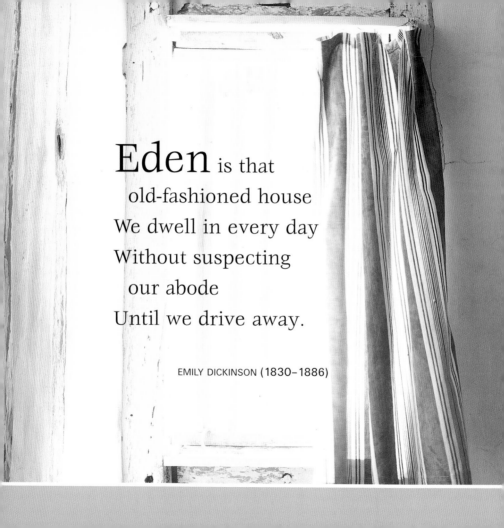

Eden is that
old-fashioned house
We dwell in every day
Without suspecting
our abode
Until we drive away.

EMILY DICKINSON (1830–1886)

Happiness

is like smallpox: if you catch it too soon, it can completely ruin your constitution.

GUSTAVE FLAUBERT (1821–1880)

Boy, take my advice, and never try to invent any thing but—happiness.

HERMAN MELVILLE (1819–1891),
THE HAPPY FAILURE

The foolish man seeks happiness in the distance; the wise grows it under his feet.

JAMES OPPENHEIM (1882–1932), *THE WISE*

Men who seek happiness are like drunkards who can never find their house but are sure that they have one.

VOLTAIRE (1694–1778)

Heap up great wealth in your house, if you wish, and live as a tyrant, but, if the enjoyment of these things be lacking, I would not buy the rest for the shadow of smoke as against happiness.

SOPHOCLES (C.497–C.406 B.C.), *ANTIGONE*

Happiness is not an
ideal of reason, but of imagination.

IMMANUEL KANT (1724–1804)

joy

The least thing precisely, the gentlest thing, the lightest thing, a lizard's rustling, a breath, a whisk, an eye-glance— little maketh up the best happiness. Hush!

FRIEDRICH NIETZSCHE (1844–1900),

THUS SPAKE ZARATHUSTRA

In the midst of happiness, one may not appreciate what happiness is.

CHINESE PROVERB

Weeping may endure for a night, but joy cometh in the morning.

THE BIBLE, PSALMS 30:5

All who joy would win
Must share it,—
Happiness was born a twin.

LORD BYRON (1788–1824), *DON JUAN*

There is no cosmetic for
beauty like happiness.

MARGUERITE, COUNTESS OF BLESSINGTON (1789–1849)

Most men pursue pleasure with such breathless haste that they hurry past it.

SØREN KIERKEGAARD (1813–1855)

Man is fond of counting his troubles, but he does not count his joys. If he counted them up as he ought to, he would see that every lot has enough happiness provided for it.

FYODOR DOSTOYEVSKY (1821–1881)

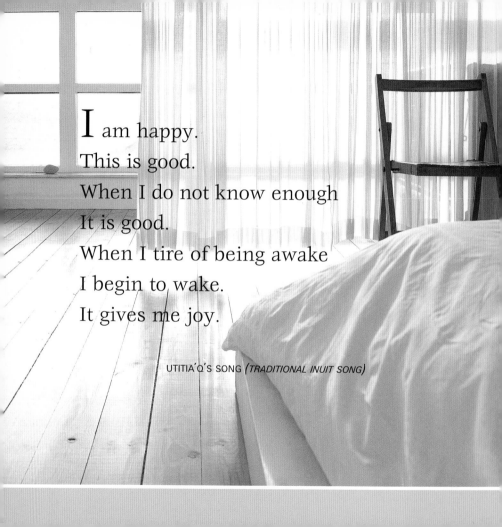

I am happy.
This is good.
When I do not know enough
It is good.
When I tire of being awake
I begin to wake.
It gives me joy.

UTITIA'Q'S SONG *(TRADITIONAL INUIT SONG)*

Fun I love, but too much fun is of all things the most loathsome. Mirth is better than fun, and happiness is better than mirth.

WILLIAM BLAKE (1757–1827)

Pleasure is very seldom found where it is sought. Our brightest blazes are commonly kindled by unexpected sparks.

SAMUEL JOHNSON (1709–1784)

We should spread joy, but, as far as we can, repress sorrow.

MICHEL DE MONTAIGNE (1533–1592)

We act as though comfort and luxury were the chief requirements in life, when all we need to make us really happy is something to be enthusiastic about.

CHARLES KINGSLEY (1819–1875)

There is only one passion, the passion for happiness.

DENIS DIDEROT (1713–1784)

One joy scatters a hundred griefs.

CHINESE PROVERB

Men's happiness and misery depends altogether as much upon their own humor as it does upon fortune.

FRANÇOIS, DUC DE LA ROCHEFOUCAULD (1613–1680)

Joy, gentle friends! Joy, and fresh days of love
Accompany your hearts!

WILLIAM SHAKESPEARE (1564–1616),
A MIDSUMMER NIGHT'S DREAM

I am too easily contented with a slight and almost animal happiness. My happiness is a good deal like that of the woodchucks.

HENRY DAVID THOREAU (1817–1862)

Crowds of bees
are giddy with clover
Crowds of grasshoppers
skip at our feet,
Crowds of larks at their
matins hang over,
Thanking the Lord for
a life so sweet.

JEAN INGELOW (1820–1897)

Pleasure is spread through the earth
In stray gifts to be claimed by whoever shall find.

WILLIAM WORDSWORTH (1770–1850), *STRAY PLEASURES*

The best way to cheer yourself up is to try to cheer somebody else up.

MARK TWAIN (1835–1910)

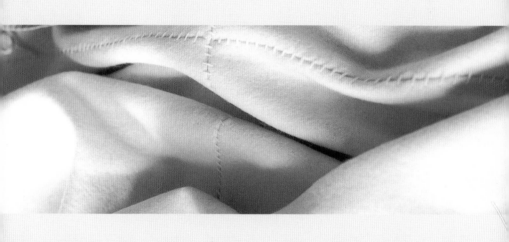

contentment

He could walk, or rather turn about in his little garden, and feel more solid happiness from the flourishing of a cabbage or the growing of a turnip than was ever received from the most ostentatious show the vanity of man could possibly invent. He could delight himself with thinking, "Here will I set such a root, because my Camilla likes it; here, such another, because it is my little David's favourite."

SARAH FIELDING (1710–1768), *THE ADVENTURES OF DAVID SIMPLE*

Happy people never count hours as they pass.

CHINESE PROVERB

Tranquil pleasures last the longest; we are not fitted to bear the burden of great joys.

CHRISTIAN NESTELL BOVEE (1820–1904)

Three grand essentials to happiness in this life are something to do, something to love, and something to hope for.

JOSEPH ADDISON (1672–1719)

People don't notice whether it's winter or summer when they're happy.

ANTON CHEKHOV (1860–1904), *THREE SISTERS*

To fill the hour,—that is happiness; to fill the hour, and leave no crevice for a repentance or an approval. We live amid surfaces, and the true art of life is to skate well on them.

RALPH WALDO EMERSON (1803–1882), *ESSAYS*

A great obstacle to happiness is to expect too much happiness.

BERNARD DE FONTENELLE (1657–1757)

The supreme happiness in life is the assurance of being loved; of being loved for oneself, even in spite of oneself.

VICTOR HUGO (1802–1885), *LES MISÉRABLES*

The essence of philosophy is that one should so live that happiness shall depend as little as possible on external things.

EPICTETUS (c.50–c.120 A.D.)

Happiness is not being pained in body or troubled in mind.

THOMAS JEFFERSON (1743–1826)

contentment

There is no greater delight than to be conscious of sincerity on self-examination.

MENCIUS (371–289 B.C.)

As on the highroad
he who walks lightest
walks with most ease,
so on the journey of
life more happiness
comes from lightening
the needs by poverty
than from panting
under a burden of
wealth.

MARCUS MINUCIUS FELIX
(2ND OR 3RD CENTURY A.D.)

Happy
is the one who
forgets that
which cannot
be changed.

GERMAN PROVERB

Nirvana is the realization of the Self; and after having once known that, if only for an instant, never again can one be deluded by the mirage of personality.

SWAMI VIVEKANANDA (1863–1902)

People are just as happy as they make up their minds to be.

ABRAHAM LINCOLN (1809–1865)

Fireside happiness,
to hours of ease
Blest with that charm,
the certainty to please.

SAMUEL ROGERS (1763–1855), *HUMAN LIFE*

O happiness! our being's end
and aim!
Good, pleasure, ease, content!
whate'er thy name:
That something still which prompts
th' eternal sigh,
For which we bear to live, or dare
to die.

ALEXANDER POPE (1688–1744), *ESSAY ON MAN*

My crown is in my heart,
  not on my head;
Not deck'd with diamonds
  and Indian stones,
Nor to be seen: my crown is
  call'd content;
A crown it is that seldom
  kings enjoy.

WILLIAM SHAKESPEARE (1564–1616), *HENRY VI PART III*

photography credits

Key: a = above, b = below, r = right, l = left

Caroline Arber 7, 8r, 35, 39, 64; Jan Baldwin 6, 9, 22, 51, 57, 61r; Christopher
Drake 10; Dan Duchars 31r; Chris Everard 26, 40, 43a; Catherine Gratwicke
13l covered box from Braemar Antiques, 13r cushion from The Housemade,
15, 19a, 27, 38 designer Caroline Zoob's home in East Sussex, 42, 43b, 44, 49,
52 Lulu Guinness' home in London, 58; Emma Lee endpapers; Tom Leighton
1, 19b, 20, 50; Jonathan Lovekin 11; Ray Main 29 client's residence, East
Hampton, New York, designed by ZG DESIGN, 34 Robert Callender &
Elizabeth Ogilvie's studio in Fife designed by John C. Hope Architects; James
Merrell 47; David Montgomery 37; Debi Treloar 16–17, 62–63; Chris Tubbs 8l,
55 Jonathan Adler's and Simon Doonan's house on Shelter Island near New
York designed by Schefer Design, 56 Phil Lapworth's treehouse near Bath;
Simon Upton 18, 60; Alan Williams 32; Andrew Wood 23 a house in London
designed by Bowles & Linares, 46 the Mogensen family's home in Gentofte,
Denmark; Polly Wreford 2–5, 12 Adria Ellis' apartment in New York, 14 & 24
Ann Shore's former home in London, 25, 28, 30–31l, 33, 45 Daniel Jasiak's
apartment in Paris, 54, 61l.

business credits

Bowles & Linares
+ 44 20 7229 9886

Lulu Guinness
www.luluguinness.com

John C. Hope Architects
+ 44 131 315 2215

Ann Shore, designer, stylist and owner of Story
Story
+ 44 20 7377 0313
Personal selection of old and new furniture and accessories. Afternoons only.

Zina Glazebrook
ZG Design
www.zgdesign.com